1

SMART
BASKETBALL
OFFICIATING

How to Get Better Every Game

by Bill Topp, *Referee* Editor and
Carl P. Schwartz, *Referee* Contributing Author

Cover design and layout by Lisa Martin
Edited by Julie Dus

Referee Enterprises, Inc., Franksville, Wis.

SMART BASKETBALL OFFICIATING:
HOW TO GET BETTER EVERY GAME
by Bill Topp and Carl P. Schwartz

Printed in the United States of America

ISBN 1-58208-025-9

Table of Contents

Introduction

Trying to learn the craft of officiating basketball from reading a book is tough during the initial stages of your career. Of course, you need to read and understand the rulebook and mechanics' manual, but there is so much more you have to learn on the court. You need game experience.

But as you gain floor experience, you stand to learn more and more from texts such as this. For example, this book exposes you to the thoughts of legendary former UCLA coach John Wooden. It's a unique perspective, coming from a coach, but one that is significant because of what Wooden has meant to the game. You'll also read chapters with NBA referees Tom Washington and Monty McCutchen, plus men's collegiate great Jim Burr.

Most of the success you will have in your career will come about because of the dealings you have with coaches and with players. Retired NBA great Jack Madden and authors Patrick Rosenow, Steven Ellinger and Brad Groninger offer their insights on that important topic.

Continue to study the rulebook and mechanics' manual, but add to your game preparations a chapter from this text each week.. You'll be better for it.

Bringing this text to you has been a team effort. *Referee* contributor Carl Schwartz and others on the *Referee* team have been instrumental in getting this text in your hands. I also want to thank the many authors and basketball greats whose thoughts grace these pages.

Bill Topp
Editor, *Referee*

1

John Wooden: An Interview

January 20, 1968: UH - 71, UCLA - 69
Houston Astrodome

Referee *knows that most true education of officials comes from officials. Whether it's a mentor relationship, regularly scheduled meetings, training sessions or postgame analysis, most referees advance their career knowledge from dealing with other officials. From time to time, you may pick up a point or gain an insight from a coach's comment or a player's request. But that's rare.*

Equally as rare is a coach such as UCLA legend John Wooden. The soon-to-be 91-year-old living in Encino, California, was interviewed for Referee *magazine in 1999. A small portion of the transcript was published in the 12/99 issue. Many readers told us they wanted more. He has much to teach you about the game, your role in the game and a plea for a return to basketball as it is meant to be. This chapter was edited in interview format based on the original transcript.*

> **"No matter what the situation is, no matter what religion, race or creed, don't think you're better than anybody is. But don't think you're not as good as anyone either."**

Referee: Why do so many people still have interest in what you have to say?

Wooden: I'm a little surprised, but let me put it this way. Had my teams not won 10 national championships, I don't believe that the interest would be there. I'd like to feel that the interest is there because of what I am as a person and not what I did as a teacher/coach.

Referee: Where did you get your dislike for the personal spotlight?

Wooden: Possibly in my very early years from my father and mother. No matter what the situation is, no matter what religion, race or creed, don't think you're better than anybody is. But don't think you're not as good as anyone either. That was Dad. He had a lot to do with my thinking.

Perhaps when I coined my own definition of success many years later, I included him saying that you can't get concerned in regard to the things over which you have no control. If you get too engrossed or involved in the things that you have no control, it will adversely affect the things over which you have control. From Dad: don't whine, don't complain, don't make excuses. Just do the best you can. Nobody can do more than that.

Referee: Let's get your overall impression about the game of basketball today.

"If you get too engrossed or involved in the things that you have no control, it will adversely affect the things over which you have control."

Wooden: As I watch the game today, I don't feel the officials are calling the game according to rules. I don't think it's the rules that need to be changed so much. I think that it's the way officials call them. Traveling is not called. Carrying the ball — players do it all the time. Moving screens, they're not called regularly.

One — once in a while. But I think officials should just call the game. I think it's just been a gradual thing. It's all changed. I think maybe society as a whole has brought the change. I talked to an NBA official a couple years ago about the traveling. He said, 'We like our jobs.' I said, 'What do you mean?' He said, 'Would you want us to call Michael Jordan for traveling when he goes in for a dunk? The fans don't want it, the people in the organization don't want it. Even the fools that complain against it — they don't want that.' I said, 'Well, why do you call it on the rookies then?'

Referee: Would the game be better if it was called exactly as it's written in the rulebook, John?

Wooden: You have to make some allowances. It can become too technical.

Referee: What about a coaching box? You didn't have a coaching box back then.

Wooden: I think coaches should stay on the bench within the bench area as long as the ball is in play. When the ball is dead, yes, they can go up to the table. But otherwise, they're all going up and down. I don't think that's good for the game. I think the fans come to see the ball game. I think television has made actors out of players, coaches and, in many cases, officials. I don't know if you agree with that or not, but I think so.

Referee: You think some officials are playing to the camera?

Wooden: I think so. Not the majority. I don't mean the majority at all, but I think definitely some. There's no question in my mind. And I would also say they might not even know they're doing it.

Let's look at the rulebook. Section 6 under general principles and the recent manual of basketball officiating is entitled, 'The Ideal Official.' That official is described as one who notices everything but is seldom noticed. He has resourcefulness and initiative. He has dignity of voice and manner and with no suggestion of pompousness. He is considerate and courteous without sacrificing firmness. He controls the players effectively and understandingly. He has constant concern for the physical, and I think you could also include mental, welfare of the players. He cooperates fully with fellow officials. He is physically able to be and is in the right place at the right time. Knows what the rules say and what the rules mean. Now that's a statement that would be very good, isn't it?

Now, a good official shall not officiate any game after having had any alcohol drink on that day nor converse with crowds at any time before, during or after game, intermissions included. Do not request to officiate games from any coach or league. No official should obligate himself to any person affiliated with any game to which he might be assigned. Not be over officious. I've seen that. Never argue with the players. Assist players in the interpretation of the rules. Also, under general impressions, use proper signals, make decisions firmly without hesitation.

Now here's what I have to say. It seems that any official who could keep reasonably close to the suggestions in the officials' books would be so nearly perfect that all coaches would be genuinely happy with his work. However, we all know that basketball is a game in which a great percentage of the calls are judgment calls. Those calls must be made almost instantaneously where the actions of unpartisan people will honestly see the action differently when the call hurts them. The very nature of the action often enables a person from a distance or from a different angle to actually see some types of infractions better than any official who may be right on top of the play. As a result, there will always be honest disagreement with many calls, as well as the highly unfair disagreements that come from blind partisanship.

The officials committee of the National Basketball Association of Coaches is working on ways to improve officiating — and the official/coach relationship. They recently asked some coaches and officials to submit a list of five things not particularly stressed that might be desirable from their own point of view. I submitted the following.

• Officials should never decide in advance how they're going to call a game or what they're going to be looking for — it's not for them to decide what they're going to be strict or lenient about.

• Officials who understand all coaches and realize that the game is a vocation for the coaches and, in most cases, is only an avocation for the officials.

• Officials who know the rules but do not hide behind the technicalities of the rulebook. The purpose of each rule should be kept in mind as well as the rule itself.

• Officials should keep all personality conflicts with coaches, players or fellow officials completely apart from anything related to the game or their officiating.

• Officials who command, rather than demand, the respect and cooperation of all those associated in any way with playing or viewing the game.

It is rather amazing how attitudes can change so much a few minutes later when the outcome of the game was to their satisfaction. The coach has a great responsibility toward the official and the official has a great responsibility toward the coach. But even more important, each should have a great responsibility toward the game in every possible respect. In the final analysis, perhaps the most important thing we need to know in all walks of life is more mutual trust, faith and understanding of the problems of others. If we acquire and keep that, the coach/official relationship would cease to be a big problem. Now I wrote that in middle '60s.

One official wrote these five suggestions:

• Keep everyone off the team bench with the exception of players in uniform, the coach and assistant coach, the trainer and one or two managers.

• Make a better effort to provide more privacy for the officials, from the coaches, players, fans, and reporters during intermission and after the game.

• Eliminate all artificial noisemakers such as horns, bells, wood blocks and so on.

• Keep the school fans away from the playing area.

• The school administrators and athletic directors should make every effort to be present at all games.

He also added the following statement: Although I do not expect my job to be easy, the coaches can help me work a better game by not calling me uncomplimentary names, not question my integrity, remaining seated on their benches, remembering that I, too, have feelings. They should not expect favors, must realize that it is possible for their players to commit infractions and realize that it is impossible for the official to see everything. But we are usually in a better position to see things than they are. I wish they would give me the kind of consideration that any man has a right to expect from another.

Referee: What problems exist between coaches and officials?

Wooden: I have become convinced that more than ever that our main problems are neither the rules nor the interpretation of the rules. Most of the serious problems seem to be the result of the administration of the rules by the officials and the lack of proper teaching of the rules by coaches. Too many of us do not teach our players to abide by the rules but look for ways to beat or get around the rules. In other words, we teach evasion of the rules and look for the technicalities that permit us to beat a rule rather than attempting to teach and live up to the spirit of the rule.

Referee: How about late in a tight game? For example, if a player makes it look good, officials are not going with an intentional foul.

> **Too many of us do not teach our players to abide by the rules but look for ways to beat or get around the rules.**

Wooden: That shouldn't have anything to do with it. There are many, many intentional fouls. I see it all the time, all the time. I saw it then, I see it now. And it's kind of like the death penalty. We'd rather free 100 guilty ones than send one not guilty to the chamber. I think we'd have a better game if it were the other way around. I think it would be a better game and we'd stop the intentional fouling if officials called more intentional fouls.

Referee: Coaches have a vocation and refs have an avocation — why do coaches keep bringing that up?

Wooden: Because something that is your vocation, you are prepared for stuff all the time. If something is your avocation, no.

Referee: But you know how refereeing is, John. It becomes a disease with officials.

Wooden: You're darn right it does. But do you have time to — do you give up your other job? To me if it's your vocation — when I played golf, I didn't play golf as good as I could play it because I had a teaching job.

Referee: But the implication in what you've said is, "I work all week long and then you (officials) come out here on a part-time basis and you can screw this up." The implication is that just because you're doing it full time, you will do whatever you're doing better than officials can referee. That seems to be a spurious correlation here. Officials can be darn good referees working three games a week.

Wooden: Sure, but couldn't you be better?

Referee: I don't know if officials would be better working five games a week.

Wooden: I think you would. Because you'd prepare yourself better. That would become a full-time job. When I said simply working a game a week, maybe I didn't mean it that way. I mean the preparation you're working all week on is what I mean. It might be doing two or three games a week and it might be doing one.

Referee: You were a basketball coach for 40 years. How many technical fouls?

Wooden: Two.

Referee: How come only two? What made you so special?

Wooden: Because I never called an official names and you never heard me use a word of profanity. I never got personal. I'd say the worse thing I ever said to an official was, and I wouldn't like somebody to say it to me if I were officiating, but I said, 'Call them the same on both ends.' I'm saying you aren't really. Or I

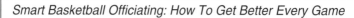

might say, 'Don't be a homer.' And I admit it. I said a moment ago I wouldn't like that.

Referee: When you got ready to play those NCAA championship games, were referees on your radar screen at all in preparation?

Wooden: I would say no, not when we got into tournament play. But, yes, in all my years I tried to get a direct reading on officials before we entered the conference season. I wanted to have two fairly tough road trips, and I liked two of those to be in the Big 10. In my career we played every school in the Big 10 back there. Couldn't get many of them to come out here. And when we played in the Big 10, for example, I'd tell my players, now, they call them different in the Big 10 and you may disagree with that, but I firmly believe it. I think that the offense gets the advantage in the Big 10. I think for charging in the Big 10, the offense is going to get the advantage most of the time. Now, that doesn't mean they're favoring the home team. We're not accustomed to it and probably won't be guilty of it as much — that's the way they call them. Now we played in Madison Square Garden a number of times. I'd say to my players, now in the East they're going to call three seconds a little closer and they're going to be a little more technical on certain areas, so we've got to accept that.

Referee: Briefly, what is the key determinant of being a successful official?

Wooden: Having a good relationship with the coaches.

Referee: You didn't say knowing the rules. You didn't say knowing the mechanics. You said having a good relationship with the coach.

Wooden: That's right. I'm assuming that you know the rules or you wouldn't be officiating.

Referee: Do you recall nights that you walked out after a game and felt that the officiating had been horrible? How did you deal with that, John?

Wooden: Yes, I just told the players that we have to put it out of our minds just as we go into it. We mustn't expect favors and we've got to put it out of our minds. That's past and it's not going to change. In many ways I talked about yesterday, today and tomorrow. You can't do a thing about the past, and the only way you can prepare for tomorrow is what you do today. I used that in various ways.

2

Success: Prepare and Present
With Jim Burr

Jim Burr

Jim Burr is a renowned men's collegiate basketball referee. He's been there. He's seen it all — done it all. Now it's his time to share some of his techniques and thoughts with you. Not all of his ideas will fit your character or your refereeing style. But read along and see what you can incorporate into your game. This chapter is based on a Referee *interview, portions of which appeared in the 2/01 issue of* Referee.

I don't know if I can define the word presence, but I've always considered myself a blue-collar referee. I'm not the best looking official and probably I'm five to 10 pounds overweight. But I think that what I've always believed in is if I give 110 percent on the court, if I hustle every time, if I try to get on every play, I think that's more important than what you want to refer to as presence. People aren't looking for my presence. They're looking for me to be in the right place at the right time to make a call that's important to them. I think that's more important.

Individual personalities

I think that 99 percent of the time, I've found that the officials all have a great amount of respect for each other. They all understand what their job is when they walk out on the court. They do the best job they can to stay in their primary areas, help out in the secondary areas. And I don't think it's any different than what I preach when I teach younger officials — you work as a team. And so I don't know if it makes much difference how much success you've had in officiating. Whether you're working an NCAA game or working a high school playoff game, I believe that if the two or three officials work as a team, just like the teams playing on the court, you're going to have more chance of success and a well-officiated basketball game.

Pregame

We're going to talk about responsibilities for the lead, the center, the trail official — what responsibilities they have. What's going to happen if we have plays coming in certain directions? How we want to rotate, how we're going to call certain plays in the game. If we do have a couple of whistles or we disagree on a call, how we're going to go about that. That is all discussed in the pregame. And I've never been in a situation where the officials, no matter what their experience level has been, haven't wanted to go out there as a crew and work the best possible game that they possibly can.

Coach and player behavior

You've got to make clear to both coaches, if they don't know you, what your line in the sand is. They've got to make sure they understand what that is. I don't believe that a coach should be working an official every single time down the court. But I think there are some legitimate times during the course of a basketball game that a coach should bring something that's concerning him to the attention of the official — no matter who it may be. And if the coach does that in a professional manner, I tell my officials that I don't think there's anything wrong with responding in a professional manner to that coach. Try to make him feel that you may not agree with it, but at least you're listening to his opinion. I think that that type of relationship back and forth between coaches and officials is certainly going to make the game a much better one to be officiated.

Changing as you gain experience

When I was a younger official, I certainly was challenged a number of times. Hopefully I stood up to those challenges. Now as the veteran official, I think it's more of my job to try and bring some of the younger officials along — trying to get the coaches to understand during the course of the game what we're trying to accomplish. I find that 95 percent of the coaches are pretty easy to work with. Sure, they disagree now and then, and gosh the game is so competitive you'd be shocked if somebody didn't disagree with you. We miss calls. There's no question about that. But if you continue to work hard — and that's the thing I try to get younger officials to understand — that you've got to put that one call that you may have a question in your mind, you've got to put it aside. If you downright think you're wrong, you've got to admit that you were wrong. But you've got to go on because the rest of the ball game must be officiated.

Helping new officials deal with veteran coaches

The first thing you do is have a real positive pregame in which that young official feels as part of the team. The younger official has certain responsibilities that he's going to have to live up to on the court. I remember myself as a young official working with some extremely good officials like Mickey Crowley and Hank Nichols. I tried to get every single call in my area right. And if there were any problems administratively during the game, I knew that those two guys would take care of them. I didn't have to worry about that. That's what I tell a young official on my crew. Listen, don't worry about the little things. If there's a problem at the table or if there's a discussion about a situation, I'll handle that. You just worry about taking care of your part of the world. Then if we get to a point where a coach is being unreasonable, I guess I try to ask the coach to back off a little bit, give the kid a chance. Let him make some bad calls before we start. I think that's one of the things that I'd like to see the coaches do — let some of the young folks get their feet wet and get in there. But there's a lack of, I guess for the lack of a better word, trust. For the coaches — until they get that feeling of trust, the young official has a difficult time and it's hard.

Getting top games

I'm a blue-collar referee. I think that I have the reputation that every single night when I go out on the court, I give them 110 percent. I try to do the very best job I possibly can. I miss calls. There's no question about that. I try to be as fair as possible. I try to adjudicate the rules the way that they're supposed to be. I try to work as hard as I can from start to finish. I try to keep my concentration. I think that's one thing that we as officials sometimes lose. And I think it's important that in the last five or six minutes of any ball game that you even get your concentration up a little bit. Sometimes if the score isn't quite where you think it should be, you lose your concentration — and that's bad. That's when officials tend to have a breakdown in communications and make mistakes. I think that if we could work more on concentration, I think we'd be better off and the game would be better officiated.

Personality in dealing with coaches

I don't really deal with any of the coaches. Basically, I really deal with the supervisors. They know that basically I'm kind of a no-nonsense guy. I have to laugh. A lot of them probably don't think I have a very good personality or that I'm kind of mad all the time. That's not really true. I think I have a very good personality. But I've been put into a situation by a conference supervisor to go out and referee a basketball game between two highly competitive individuals on the sidelines who both want to win. I've got to somehow run that game using the rules of basketball and rules of common sense to make sure that both of them have a fair opportunity to win the game. To me, that is not a very easy job. Some guys go about it in different ways. I go about it as a business, as a blue-collar referee that goes to the game to do his job. Sometimes I probably come across that way — as maybe being too much of a hard-ass. To me, that is the only way that I can get the job done in a successful manner. I certainly don't mean to come across the wrong way, but to me that's the job description that I feel I have. That's how I have to go about doing it to get the job done.

Players' respect

I don't know if the players at the major college level are as concerned with the officiating as the coaches are. Some of them are. I think the players are terrific kids. They're 20-year-old college kids that are playing a great game. They are going through a real fine time in their life. And I don't know if there is a concern about the officiating. Not as much as the coaches are who are over there trying to orchestrate those guys to perform.

Scheduling games

I feel that I have a very good relationship with the supervisors of officials in each of the conferences. And during most of my career, since the beginning of the Big East Conference, I have given my first allegiance to the Big East Conference. They brought me along as a young official. They had faith in me when I screwed up and stuck with me, and I kept coming. So I think there's a certain loyalty that I have to the conference because of that. So I basically deal with them first and their supervisor of officials. Then I go to the other leagues and try to be as evenly divided amongst those assignors as I possibly can. And there are also times when a supervisor will ask me to take a particular game. I could go back to the Big East and request a certain date or something. And if it can be worked out, it's great. If that supervisor feels that that game is a little bit too important as far as he's concerned, he'll just say no, and I handle it as such.

To me it's a business, and I deal with those guys up front. Once in a while they get upset, but once in a while I get upset. It happens, but basically it all works out. I try to work as many leagues as possible because I enjoy the basketball in all the leagues. They're very competitive games. And the inter-conference games are very competitive. I like that competitiveness which, to me, brings the competitiveness out of the officiating crew to the point of trying to do a good game in that competitive nature.

Bench decorum

I think officials are handling bench decorum well. I think we've gotten better. I think from that aspect that we've done a better job as the coaches begin to understand what our positions are. And there're certain nights we are not in the best of moods or things aren't going our way. Generally I think the officials are making an effort to understand what the coach is going through. One thing that I preach at my camps and talk to my guys is —as you come up the officiating ranks, it's good to also understand what a coach goes through. I've learned being a supervisor of officials for a Division III basketball conference, because I talk to a lot of athletic directors and coaches, and I kind of get a drift of what they're going through. Then all of a sudden some official like me walks into the court and they don't see eye to eye. So I think it's good for officials to learn a little bit about what a coach goes through — practices, schedule, being on the road. They will have a little bit of a tolerance and understanding of what a coach is going through, too. I'm not so sure that should make a difference in how an official referees a basketball game, but the more you understand about everybody's personality involved, I think the better off you are if you have a situation that you have to handle.

The Division I game

We're getting better. I think we have a long ways to go. I think we've been weak in whistling illegal screens. I think we've been weak in calling the 'chucking the cutter' plays. And I know that is an area that I need to work on, and it's hard. I think it will be an absolute constant battle in college basketball officiating, now and long after I'm gone, to continually work on the lead and center officials not to follow the ball. And I think that that's probably one of the great things the NBA has done. They've gotten their officials to stay in their area, look off the ball in their area — those guys have done an outstanding job. I think it's something we have to continue to work on in college officiating. It's a mental thing, and it's a hard habit to break. If I were a young official today, I would work harder at concentrating looking off the ball and having a peripheral look at where the ball is. But I would work on not following the ball 100 percent of the time. I think that's one of the big things that we have to continually teach officials.

Consulting referees on mechanics changes

I'd like to see the supervisors come to us before they make drastic mechanics changes. I remember seven or eight years ago when they wanted to make a significant change in the rotation. We met before the season and we tried it out. We worked on it and we talked about it, and it's worked out really well. It was a smart way to handle it. But now all of a sudden we have some mechanics changes that no one has ever come to us and asked our opinion. The officials sometimes might not feel that is the best thing for us while we're out there. But I don't think we should have anything to say as far as representation on the rules committee. That's not our job. I think our job is to use those rules the way they want their game refereed and go out on the court and do it.

3

Never Stop Learning

By Tom Washington

The NFL. The NHL. MLS. MLB. The NBA. That alphabet soup indicates you've reached the top of the heap. One of the men who reached that esteemed height shares some lessons learned along the way. If you have experience, share it by becoming a mentor. If you need some help, ask someone to serve as your mentor. There are many tips on how to accomplish that within Washington's column.

This chapter is based on columns submitted by NBA referee Tom Washington, Referee's Doing It *columnist for 2000-01. Thanks to NBA director of officiating Ed T. Rush and the NBA for sharing the league's officiating knowledge with our readers.*

Mentoring: A Constant State of Learning

Throughout our lifetime we should be in a constant state of learning. We take each day and take the experiences and add them to our books of knowledge. The books become volumes and the volumes make up our libraries. The project at hand should be to build a massive library of references, a library to which we can refer when needed to handle the challenges that arise. Refereeing is much like every other area of life. You must constantly stay refreshed to stay updated to the changes that "life" and "the game" brings. Establish your libraries and update your information constantly.

Once we establish our libraries, we should open the doors to everyone so that we can share that knowledge. Get out and visit other libraries. Much like the growth process of children becoming adults, students become teachers and followers become leaders. Wealthy is the man or woman who shares his or her wealth. Poor is the man or woman who hoards his or her gold.

Mentoring is "reach one and teach one." Mentoring is also "reach me and teach me." The most valuable asset we can give is ourselves. We should give sincerely, impartially and freely with no expectations in return. Time, which we all value so dearly, is priceless. Taking the time to give your time is a gift that can never be repaid. If there is a goal to be met in that process, it should be to give the best qualities we have to improve those around us. In doing so, we can build better leaders in life.

In the officiating world, that means officials become head referees or crew chiefs. That promotes the best service that we can offer on the floor, for the best game possible.

Begin

Pick up the telephone and call someone and talk basketball. Sit down and watch a game tape with a fellow official. Sit down and watch a game or two with your co-workers and/or peers in the industry. Do that with total disregard to age, gender and experience.

Sometimes you have to take the first step in order to help others. I challenge everyone to find someone to reach out to help him or her with their officiating. Ask them what their goals are and how they plan to obtain them. Help develop a plan of success. Give your experiences to them to help in that area. Offer to review a few game films with them and whenever possible go to watch them work in person. Get to know your "mentorees" on a personal level so that you can effectively assess their "referee personality." Help develop an oncourt personality. You need to know the person in order to know the referee.

Help develop a plan of success. Give your experiences to them to help in that area.

Set up study groups or sessions to reinforce the rules knowledge. Last, but not least, teach by example. Show by your actions what to do. Be a professional on and off the court. Value what you do with a humbling pride. Be not boastful, but hold your head high so that others may see and learn. One important note here is that in no way does being a "mentor" elevate you above someone. It should actually humble you so that you too can learn during the process. It is actually a way to become more rooted and centered.

Learn to listen

Learn to see. Do so with a critiquing nature, not a critical one. If you never shared what you know with someone then you are being selfish and self-serving. At some point in your career you must become a teacher. Ask yourself at this very moment: Do I have something to offer to someone? Can I elevate someone with what I know? Can't answer "yes" to those questions? Then you need to reassess what you are doing and get to work!

Do I have something to offer to someone? Can I elevate someone with what I know?

Those of you who seek the help, be willing to accept someone's invitation to do the things mentioned above. Set aside your pride and open your mind. Look to someone to learn from at some time. What I wish to emphasize here is that we are all "mentorees." Seek out a mentor. Don't be afraid to ask to be fed some knowledge. If you are truly hungry — eat! Experience level doesn't matter either.

Some of you will be better mentors (teachers) but you all continue to learn. Take the time to make a game tape available for review by someone other than yourself. Go to a sports bar or a friend's home and watch a game together and review the plays. Share your game experiences. Lay them out for discussion. Encourage dialogue. It's OK to bare your soul! Challenge each other to elevate each other. Seek the higher ground. Always be willing to reach a level of understanding and make sure your partners reach that same level.

One aspect of learning is teaching

Teaching allows not only the students to be able to gain knowledge but allows the teachers to be able to reinforce their skills. The act of mentoring is to be able to reach out to someone and share one's knowledge and skills. Let someone share in your experiences. Mentoring, in its simplest form, is reaching out to someone and sharing your knowledge. Take the responsibility of someone much in the same manner that a father or mother does with his or her child. By doing so you can help your fellow official and help yourself in the process. The rewards are priceless and endless. Do so in a truly giving and unselfish manner. Give everyone his or her due respect. Though you wish to nurture like you do our children, by no means treat anyone like a child. Think of the process in that manner. View yourself as a cup willing to be filled with water. Those waters represent knowledge. Once that cup is filled, it is ready to quench someone's thirst. Let that be done and give until they are satisfied. Once the cup begins to empty it can now be refilled with more water. The process is endless.

I issue this challenge to all officials: Fill the cup with water to quench someone's thirst. And to those who are thirsty — seek the water.

PROFESSIONALISM

"Professionalism is an understanding that each official must be the game's most meaningful ambassador both on the court and in the community. It entails having a quality approach, both on and off the court, that is a credit to the game and to the profession of basketball officiating." That remarkable statement is found at the front of the *NBA Officials' Manual*. I believe you can apply it to whatever level you are officiating. You always represent the entire community of officials. The work you perform is not only a reflection of yourself but of every official. For many of your friends, family and acquaintances, you are the only official they know and may ever know. As unfair as it may seem, it is a fact:

They will judge all officials by what you do. Are you willing to accept the responsibility?

Each game deserves your maximum effort. No matter what level of play you are officiating, no matter what the score may be or the time remaining in the game, you must have a dedicated purpose. Enjoy your work, but always take it seriously. Take pride in each game and assist others whenever possible. Treat the crew as one entity and take pride and responsibility for everything it does each night.

Are you willing to accept the responsibility?

Professionalism is one aspect of being prepared mentally. Officials must always remember that they are in the public eye both on the court and off. That goes along with the perils and perks of officiating. We are recognized for what we do but must remember that we are accountable for who we are. The uniforms we wear allow the world to hold us to a higher standard. If you are not willing to accept that responsibility, I suggest you do something else.

On the court

Oncourt professionalism begins with your arrival at the gym. When you arrive, you will make a first impression. You should be dressed accordingly. For example, we all have worked at the neighborhood recreational center and, generally, you can arrive dressed in your uniform. However, your uniform "look" is important. Being disheveled, as if you just dressed out of the trunk of the car, is unprofessional. Look as if you know what you are doing and you care. At higher levels you should arrive at the game, at a minimum, in business-casual attire. No one ever made a bad first impression by wearing a jacket and tie. Remember this: You may not receive credit for being dressed appropriately, but you will receive criticism for being dressed inappropriately.

Sounds like the game itself: You may not get credit for getting the call right, but if you miss it, you will be criticized.

Once you are at the game and are ready to work, another part of being professional involves interacting with your partner. Give your partner the same, if not more, respect that you would like to receive. Understand that everyone is there to do a job and that everyone should have come totally prepared. It is important to set aside egos. Everyone has to participate in the pregame. Every voice has the right to be heard with respect. No matter what your experience level, you should be involved either by asking questions or answering them. You can never be too prepared. Feel free to discuss the obvious. Attention to detail can make the difference.

Often, in preparing for a game, it helps to go back to the basics. The basics are the things we take for granted and feel silly about even mentioning. They are so simple and obvious. For example: "Referee the defense; know your primary areas; hustle on every play, and always elevate your concentration levels." That is why pregame routines are important. They give you a chance to discuss situations with your partners that they have experienced or can offer insight into. By doing so, you enrich yourself and reinforce your knowledge and ability to handle floor situations.

Once you have prepared yourself for the game, the "game plan" must be executed. Work on the floor as if it is your first and last game. In your first game, you probably couldn't have been more enthusiastic (or more scared), and in your last game, you hope to make everyone remember you as a great referee. Take that pride and lace it with enthusiasm. Every call is important to the game; therefore, take pride in your calls. Show confidence, but not arrogance. Never sit on information that can help your crew be the best it can be. Step up and take responsibility.

Offcourt professionalism

What is your role in the community? Are you a leader there as well? How are you perceived when traveling? It's easy to believe that once the game is over, no one remembers you, but that is far from the truth. It's easy to say the world only remembers the shirts we wear, but it's not always true. Often you are remembered and held to a higher standard. Accept that fact. Your integrity is the one quality you can never compromise. Officials are role models. Take pride in that. Serve your community in some capacity. There are so many possibilities.

You are also an ambassador when you travel, whether by plane, train or automobile or walking around the corner. Remember that you are a representative of the entire officiating community. Help us all by being the best you can be at all times. Be proud of who you are and of being a referee.

(Tom Washington, Laverock, Pa., has been an NBA referee since 1991. He began his career at the high school level.)

4

Are You
Fired Up?

BRIAN SPURLOCK

Basketball officials should be fired up to take the floor when game time arrives. Perhaps that fire comes from within. The NBA's Monty McCutchen and former Referee *columnist Brad Groninger remind you why we do what we do.*

The Craftsman
By Monty McCutchen

From where does the first pulse of passion originate for the referee? Is it the smell of the gym that takes you back to a simpler time in the past? Is it the competition that burns in you long after the talent to play leaves? Is it the camaraderie that develops into lifetime friendships? Is it a sense of fairness in a world in which fairness often takes a backseat to winning at all costs? Or is it the game itself that calls you to serve in a role that requires a special personality to survive in? Whatever the reasons that called you to become one of those that are loathed, you must know that it is an honorable craft.

There are as many routes to success in this crazy business of officiating as there are joys that arise out of its pursuit. As basketball officials, we find ourselves smack dab in the middle of the greatest game ever invented (I whole-heartedly admit to my bias) and I am left to ponder about how one might achieve both that success and joy simultaneously.

Maybe your uncle knew Irv Brown and set up a lunch meeting where all your refereeing questions, past, present and forever more were answered. Maybe your dad worked a game with Dick Callahan at the Palestra in Philadelphia in the late '60s, when working at the Palestra for officials paralleled starting in center field for the Yankees. There you were, a young snotty-nosed kid, listening in on the masters talking about the game and to this day memories of that night still resonate. Maybe Mendy Rudolph stopped in at the local YMCA game you were working, liked how you handled the volunteer clock operator's myriad of mistakes and then gave you what all officials need at some point — time with someone who knows more than you know.

For me, the secrets of refereeing and the road to achieving my goal of becoming a NBA official came from the source of wisdom that I continually find myself going back to time and again — my father. Although he never refereed, like many fathers he showed me the path that would lead to rewarding experiences within the craft.

I had just returned from my first refereeing camp, and at 21 years old I hardly would classify my experience as a success — except in one area. I knew a passion had seized me and would not let go any time soon. As only a parent could, my father knew I had found what made me happy.

"So you think this is what you would like to do, is it?" he asked.

"I've never felt more at home, Dad, as when I'm on the floor working a game," I responded.

"Well then, listen closely because you need to hear this," he continued. "There once was a young man not far from your age who lived in New York City at the turn of the century. He came across another man with an old grizzled face who was preparing to climb what seemed to be an infinite set of scaffolding toward the top of this new skyscraper being built. The scaffolding creaked and groaned at the weight of the man and the young man couldn't help but ask, 'Sir, aren't you afraid to go so high on such old and shaky scaffolding?' 'Not at all young fellow, because I'm the one who built this scaffolding.' Monty, if you're going to do this, do it right and build yourself a good set of scaffolding that will support you no matter how high it takes you."

Then and there I knew I would never get a better set of words to live by.

It is the pursuit of the craft that made the ability to call officiating a career possible. Most importantly, however, it is the pursuit of the craft that insured I would enjoy the process along the way. By focusing on the foundation that is constantly being laid, one layer at a time, I hope to continue to grow regardless of the amount of years I am fortunate enough to call this job my own.

Nothing is as sweet as learning something from a partner in the middle of the third quarter in a small gym in the midst of a South Dakota winter while working a CBA game with 84 screaming basketball degenerates (which I gladly count myself as one) in the stands. Nothing is as sweet as nailing a play in the second quarter of a junior high girls' game because you want to honor the game and do your job right night in and night out. It is like hitting the sweet spot in your three iron on the approach to the 18th green (not that I would know anything about that). Nothing is as comforting as walking on the floor knowing you have the tools to handle anything that arises. Nothing is as rewarding as enjoying a fellow referee's advancement, because you have enough confidence in your own impending or past success.

> **Nothing is as comforting as walking on the floor knowing you have the tools to handle anything that arises.**

The craftsman knows those joys and more. The craftsman's focus is where it should be — on the game, on the craft, on the passion that drew him there in the first place and most importantly on the eternal pursuit of bettering who he is and what he has chosen to give himself up to.

But there are pitfalls along the way that every official must navigate in order to be a craftsman. It is far too easy to want quick and instant success over a time-consuming craft; to resent others' good fortune and accuse them of political behavior; to start looking at the checks instead of the games being worked; and to blame the supervisor or assignor for lack of improvement or movement. But those thoughts are wasted energy; they keep us from truly moving forward into the realm of the craftsman. How do you know if you are honoring the craft? For me, I try to continually ask myself the following questions:

• Do I listen to my partners — both those with more and less experience than me, for knowledge comes in many forms? Often it is a question from someone else that shows you a weakness in your own game.

• Do I defend my position when questioned by a supervisor or a more experienced referee, or do I open myself up to what is being said in the hopes of learning something valuable?

• Do I break my game down without being asked, or do I hope no one notices the plays and situations I have questions about? Do I take those questions to the individuals who might have the answers or am I afraid of being thought less of because I'm not perfect?

• Do I know my rulebook so that it is as much a part of me as breathing? Do I know it enough that no participant can put doubt in my mind in relation to the rules of the game?

• Do I care about the games, all the games, on my schedule equally?
Do my partners like seeing my name on their schedule?

• Am I willing to fail and learn from my failures?

• Am I willing to help others get better, without fearing they will take something from me?

• Most importantly, do I love the game?

For me, living up to those questions is the barometer that allows me to feel comfortable as I move forward toward my goals. If I can answer those questions truthfully and with an unwavering voice, I know that the career I seek will fall in line like a dutiful soldier. D.H. Lawrence, the great English writer, said it best when he wrote:

"There is no point in work
   Unless it absorbs you
   Like an absorbing game.
   If it doesn't absorb you
   If it's never any fun
   Don't do it."

Go forward with the eye on the craft and let the games you are a part of absorb you, and what you seek you will find. To the craftsman in all of us, do well.

(Monty McCutchen has been officiating in the NBA since 1992. He resides in Pipe Creek, Texas. This article first appeared in the 6/01 issue of Referee.*)*

NEW YEAR'S RESOLUTIONS
By Brad Groninger

Just as many of us pledge our New Year's resolutions while the ball is literally dropping at Times Square, let us also begin another basketball season with a full slate of new season's resolutions. After all, the bouncing of the basketball marks the beginning of yet another new year. Here are a few suggestions:

I resolve to get in shape physically.
Some sort of cardiovascular activity should be part of your daily preseason conditioning. Walking, jogging or running goes a long way to bringing the heart rate to levels approaching those necessary to run effortlessly up and down the court for the next four months.

I resolve to get in shape mentally.
The few weeks just prior to the season opener should be devoted to reacquainting yourself with the rulebook, the officiating manual and the handbook provided by your state association or

assigning body. Plan to spend some serious time studying both the literal application and spirit of the rules.

I resolve to confirm my game assignments and contracts.

Correspond with each and every athletic director concerning your upcoming schedule. A simple postcard or phone call to the athletic director can save you a lot of anguish and embarrassment down the road. Confirm the year's schedule in one sitting. Do it now and get it done. Sign and return all contracts to the appropriate assigning body.

I resolve to update my personal information with my supervisor and assignors.

Take a look at the roster information you provided your secretary in the spring and summer. Has any address change been provided? Have any telephone area codes changed since last season? Who can I provide my new pager number, fax number or cellular number?

I resolve to replenish my supply of officiating equipment and take an inventory of everything in my officiating bag.

Check your referee clothing for holes, soiled or faded spots, loose hem lines, weak seams, rusted or broken zippers and frayed shoe strings. Invest a little money in your tools. Replace worn shoes and broken whistles. Stock your officiating gear with toothpaste, mouthwash, hair spray, aspirin, safety pins and nail clippers. Leave nothing for granted.

I resolve to work my fair share of scrimmages.

It is unrealistic to begin the season in peak form. We need to utilize practices and scrimmages to hone our mechanics, judgment and concentration levels. Don't just show up and go through the motions in order to take the opportunity to politic with the coaches. Work the scrimmage like you would work an ordinary game. Don't think that just because the gym is empty you are not being watched. Set a good example for your partners.

I resolve to communicate with my partner(s) at the beginning of each week.

Take a Sunday evening and call your officiating partners for the week, arranging plans for travel and arrival times. Plan to share a ride, if possible; 30 to 90 minutes in the car together can provide a suitable forum for some valuable pregame discussions.

I resolve to evaluate myself on videotape.

All of us have the opportunity today to secure videotape of our basketball games. Throw a blank tape or two in your bag for that moment when the athletic director concedes to make available a copy of the game tape. But don't just tape the game and watch it. You can be your own best critic. Watch the tape with a critical eye. Look for ways to improve your court presence. Ask yourself some tough questions. Did I hustle? Was I in position to make the tough call? Do I sell my calls to players, coaches and partners?

I resolve to arrive at the game site on time.

To be on time is to be late. To be early is to be on time. Don't cause the game administration undo worry. Arrive in plenty of time to relax from your road trip. Give yourself time to prepare mentally for the work ahead. Familiarize yourself with the facility and schedule. If there is another game in progress, watch those officials work, or hang around afterwards and watch the more experienced officials work the varsity game. Ask questions and listen.

I resolve to conduct a meaningful pregame conference.

The length of the conference is not nearly as important as the content of the conference. A power-packed 10-minute discussion of rules and mechanics is far more important and relevant than 30 minutes of ego-stroking, back-biting and one-upsmanship. Use that time to your advantage. Don't wait for things to happen. Take the bull by the horn and lead the pregame discussions.

I resolve to use proper mechanics.

Find out how your supervisor or assignor prefers you to work concerning style and mechanics. Don't be tempted to adopt a mechanic you've seen used on television just because it looked cool. Follow the prescribed mechanics and signals and you can't go wrong.

I resolve to strive for total concentration.

You cannot afford to let your mind wander during the course of the game. Discipline yourself to focus on the players, coaches, and your partner(s). The one time you allow yourself to mentally relax is the one time you find yourself ankle deep in controversy. Anticipate situations before they happen and react to them with poise and confidence.

I resolve to honestly evaluate my efforts each night.

Don't fall into the trap of working night after night without some serious self-evaluation.

I resolve to have fun.

If the enjoyment and fulfillment of officiating has vanished, it is time to pass the torch. Strive to work hard, but understand it is a game. Rekindle the enthusiasm you brought to the table when you first began officiating.

I resolve to act in a professional manner.

From the time I sign my contract until the time I endorse the check, I pledge to represent basketball officials everywhere in only the highest light. My thoughts, actions and speech will be representative of a true professional. I will wear my striped shirt proudly.

It is one thing to merely make resolutions. It is quite another to follow through with them. As you venture into another basketball season, don't just give lip-service to those promises. Put the resolutions to practice.

(Brad Groninger is a college basketball official from Muncie, Ind. This article originally appeared as a basketball Doing It in Referee's *12/98 issue.)*

5

First Talk,
Then 'T'

DALE TAIT

Smoke and mirrors. Humor. Hustle. A smile. Those and a dozen more things lead to good game control.

Longtime Referee *contributor Steven Ellinger offers insights from years on the floor. Ellinger talks about traits that good officials exhibit on the floor, but stresses that each confrontation has an ending point. Being able to walk that tightrope is going to lead to future success in your career.*

When a player or coach crosses the line you've set, you need to take care of business. U.S. Air Force judge Patrick Rosenow talks about giving the needed technical. Technical fouls, in and of themselves, aren't bad. Perhaps it is the way those technical fouls are called, communicated and administered. Read along as retired NBA great Jack Madden shares the lesson he learned, the hard way, about properly taking care of business. Madden learned to make those tense situations more palatable — and with that lesson, his career blossomed.

What Do Good Officials have in Common?
By Steven Ellinger

Successful basketball officials have excellent rules knowledge, they understand the intent of the rules and they use the proper mechanics. However, impeccable rules knowledge and mastering the prescribed mechanics are not surefire keys to an official's success. It is equally important to have good people skills and know how to communicate with the different personnel you will encounter during a game. Watch successful officials in person and on television. What characteristic do they have in common? They are all good communicators.

Every local officials association has members who have mastered the rules, use the proper mechanics and then fail to improve their schedule and move up the ladder. Invariably, they blame it on politics. Those people should instead look at their communication skills. More likely than not, being a bad communicator is impeding their progress. Successful officials understand that their appearance, manner and voice often determine how they are accepted. They know how to use verbal skills, when to use them and use them well in communicating and developing a good rapport with players, coaches, table personnel and, most importantly, fellow officials.

Officials who have rules knowledge, good judgment and make good decisions, but who cannot communicate effectively with others are doomed to fail. If they cannot communicate effectively with coaches and their fellow officials, no one will recognize that they possess good rules knowledge, have good judgment and make good decisions.

Why is developing communication skills so important in officiating? Those skills go a long way in controlling a game and defusing potentially difficult situations. Good communication between partners, players and coaches is a two-way street and can be the difference between a smooth-running game and a potentially disastrous one.

At least half of the problems officials have in games results from faulty communications. Have you ever been in a game when a failure to communicate with your partner at a critical moment led to chaos? What about situations when a coach just had to talk to you — you ignored the coach and the game went downhill from there?

What are the essentials for developing good communication skills? To start with, you must have common sense, be friendly and be businesslike. Your voice should be loud enough to be heard but not challenging. Used positively, your voice can help you keep control of a game.

Communication skills entail more than just speaking well. Successful officials are approachable and are good listeners. They recognize that they have two ears and one mouth — and they use them in that proportion. Coaches and players are turned off by officials who appear unapproachable or standoffish. An official may feel he is approachable, however, if he is perceived by a coach as being unapproachable, then he probably is unapproachable. With perception being 90 percent of reality, whether the perception is in fact accurate is not important. Coaches will believe what they want to believe, and if they believe you are a poor official, for whatever reason, then you are a poor official — at least in that coach's eyes. On the other hand, if a coach feels you are a good official, you will often get the benefit of the doubt, even if there are disagreements with some of your calls.

Successful officials also understand the difference between being self-confident and cocky. Cockiness has no place in officiating. A cocky official might say to a coach, "That's the call I made. Now sit down. I don't want to hear anymore." A confident official would instead say, "Coach, I saw the whole play and there was no contact." Remember that it is not what you say but rather the manner in which you say it. Successful officials treat others like they would like to be treated. They are courteous, and they are neither arrogant nor boastful.

Communicating also goes beyond words, and includes body language and signals.

Communicating also goes beyond words, and includes body language and signals. Officials convey messages with their posture, gestures, facial expressions, movements and the tone of their voice. Signals are the most important part of an official's "language." They are an official's way of telling others what is going on in a game. Good signals demonstrate decisiveness and can even cause a borderline or possibly a wrong call to be accepted.

Communicating with partners.
Before you ever get to the game site, communicate with your partner. Contacting your partner prior to the game to confirm the

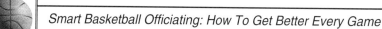

game time, game site and travel arrangements will often prevent your partner from being a no-show because of a possible schedule mix-up. Assignment secretaries and commissioners do make mistakes. Just ask someone in your local association about the time they arrived at an alleged game site and the only people they encountered were maintenance personnel.

A pregame conference is especially important when working with a new partner, whether that partner is a veteran or a rookie. Key areas of communication during the pregame conference include working out of your primary area, handling conflicting calls, maintaining consistency and handling changing calls.

On the court, eye contact is an effective means of communicating with your partner. After all, your partner should be the first to know what the call is, shouldn't he? Partners should use each other to make the administration of fouls and penalties flow smoothly with minimal errors, such as pointing each other toward the correct basket when administering a technical foul.

Have you ever witnessed a play where there was no eye contact, resulting in a wrong call? It happens! How about a double whistle on a play with one official signaling a block while the other official signals a player-control foul?

How about communication between partners when the ball crosses the end line and the responsible official is unsure which player caused the ball to go out of bounds? That is not the time for the other official to discretely point direction. A quick yell, decisive signal, brief words or even a face-to-face discussion may be necessary to get the call right.

What about out-of-bounds plays when one partner changes the other's call? In almost all cases, only out-of-bounds calls and incorrect rule interpretations should be changed, and then, only obvious mistakes should be corrected. The helping official must see the entire play clearly in order to offer an opinion and must be 100 percent certain that the calling official is wrong before offering a suggested change. Being 99 percent sure is not sufficient. Choice of words is very important in those situations. Do not ask your partner, "Did you see the whole play?" or "Did you get a good look at the play?"

Ever have a partner admit they guessed and did not see the entire play? The phrase, "I think the ball last touched number 24" is not acceptable. "I clearly saw the ball go out of bounds when last touched by number 24" is the better way to offer assistance. Do not tell your partner it is the gold team's ball or the red team's ball. Ask instead, "Did you see the gold player tip the ball after the red player touched it?" Tell your partner what you saw — give him information — and then give him the opportunity to change the call. If an incorrect call is made, the official who made the original call should make the change, not the helping official.

One more caveat about changing calls: Make sure that changing a call will have a positive impact on the game. Remember, your primary objective is to get the call right. If you cannot do that, the next best thing is to have a good, strong wrong call.

Never, though, criticize a partner publicly. If you have a problem with a fellow official, deal with it privately.

The better you communicate with your partners, the better you will work as a team. Never, though, criticize a partner publicly. If you have a problem with a fellow official, deal with it privately. Remember — if you cannot say anything nice about a fellow official, at least be vague.

Communicating with table personnel.
Treat table personnel politely and with respect. Make them feel like they are an important part of the game. Thank table personnel for their assistance toward the end of the game. If you only recognize table personnel when problems occur, you will not get high marks for game management. At the sub-varsity

level, table personnel may often have many more years of experience than the officials. Yet sometimes table personnel do not know if the ball is stuffed or inflated. Table personnel can be a tremendous help or a big hindrance. They can often be the difference between a smooth-flowing game and one filled with glitches.

Before the game, give instructions to table personnel and create rapport. Discuss how to handle substitutions, when to switch the alternating possession arrow, how to handle correctable errors, handling scorebook discrepancies, putting team foul totals on the scoreboard and when to turn on the bonus light on the scoreboard.

Eye contact also comes into play when communicating with the scorer's table. Permitting substitutes to enter the game, knowing when a team is in the bonus situation and glancing at the scorer's table prior to handing the ball to the free-throw shooter are three instances when eye contact or non-verbal communication with the table personnel could prevent awkward situations.

During timeouts, if you are close to the scorer's table, that might be a good opportunity to inquire how many more fouls before a team is in the bonus situation, remaining timeouts, etc. Do not hang around the table during all timeouts. There are no game assignments given out at the scorer's table, and table personnel will not tell you what a wonderful job you are doing.

Communicating with yourself.

Talking to yourself may cause you to receive strange looks from others in everyday life, but it can be extremely effective during a game — just keep lip movement to a minimum.

Talking to yourself helps you anticipate free-throw violations, basket interference, goaltending, and prepares you for the unexpected so that you are not caught by surprise. Reminding yourself of the time remaining, knowing the number of team fouls and recalling previously-assessed warnings will assist you in anticipating those situations when they do occur.

Rules knowledge and utilizing the proper mechanics are expected of officials and only get noticed when they are glaringly absent. Communication skills are an important part of the successful official. Developing good communication skills and using them to your advantage are an integral part of an official's success.

Taken from another perspective, view your officiating career as a bank account. The more money you deposit in the account by the positive images and good communication skills you possess and convey, the less of an impact a withdrawal has at the times you mess up and say something you should not.

KNOW WHEN TO SAY WHEN

If you want to make the game better, there must be communication between coaches and officials. Keep in mind three principles when dealing with coaches: know what to say, know when to say it and know whom you can say it to.

Before the game, be friendly yet businesslike when dealing with coaches. Answer legitimate questions and respond to concerns. Do not dodge questions — the longer you ignore questions, the longer they last. Keep pregame conversations professional and brief; those conversations are not opportunities to conduct rules clinics. Do not be overly friendly, particularly if you have known one coach for a lengthy period of time but have never encountered the other coach.

During the game, if a coach questions a play, try responding: "Coach, here's what I saw...." Another approach might be to acknowledge that a play might have actually happened the way the coach described it and that you might have missed it. With that type of response, you are just acknowledging that you might be wrong, not that you were in fact wrong.

Are you tired of listening to a coach? Try, "Coach, I have heard enough;" "I hear you;" or "I will look." Hard as it may sometimes be, be pleasant in those situations and do not put coaches on the defensive or attempt to intimidate them.

If a coach complains about a player camping in the lane, which response is most effective? Acknowledging the statement with a nod of the head? Ignoring the statement? Or responding, "No way, coach. He's been fine all night." Most of the time, ignoring that type of statement or acknowledging it with a simple nod of the head will end the matter. However, when you defend your position, the coach instinctively feels defensive and then goes on the offensive, continuing the dialogue.

As long as a question or statement is made in a respectful manner, listen to the coach and then respond if appropriate. Remember, though, that not every statement or question merits a response. Before responding, ask yourself if responding to the coach will do more harm than good. Coaches will react positively if they believe you are willing to listen to them. Besides, you do not have to do what coaches want you to do. A simple "I'll watch for that" often works wonders. Coaches want to know that you are working with them, not against them, and that you are willing to listen.

When dealing with coaches, never get mad, shout or lose your cool. Shouting indicates a loss of control — of both yourself and the game.

If you speak to one coach during the game, invite the other coach to join the conversation. Those invitations are great conversation minimizers!

When dealing with coaches, never get mad, shout or lose your cool. Shouting indicates a loss of control — of both yourself and the game. There is never a valid excuse for losing your cool, regardless of what is happening in the game. Officials are hired to maintain control of the game, and they cannot do that if they cannot maintain control of themselves. Work on maintaining an even keel in emotionally charged situations.

Never use vulgarity and never threaten coaches. Avoid "if, ... then" statements, such as "If you say one more word, then it's a technical foul." If the coach then responds with, "I'm sorry," you are in a box. The coach apologized, but said two words, not one. What are your choices? Accept the apology and not follow through with the threat, or assess a technical foul, even though the coach apologized. Either way, you lose. If a situation is serious enough to warrant a threat, it is probably serious enough to penalize without invoking the threat.

Don't know how to respond to a coach? Don't say anything. Silence cannot come back to haunt you, and it cannot be quoted.

Never embarrass a coach in front of the players and also recognize that you are not beyond making mistakes. Try to minimize mistakes and recognize that it is OK to make mistakes. Just make sure you are making new mistakes. If you keep making the same mistakes, you will not improve, regardless of how good your communication skills are.

Even successful officials make mistakes.

What makes them successful, however, is that they have achieved their success through repetition. They officiate many games, they see the same type of plays and eventually they get them right. Above all, successful officials are good communicators.

Some no-nos when dealing with coaches: Don't ever say, "It wasn't my call." The coach's response? "It obviously wasn't your partner's call either." If you observe a play and do not feel a call is necessary, say so if there is an opportunity. Responding to a coach's complaint, "You coach and I'll referee," will invite the comment from the coach, "OK, when are you going to start?"

Following the game, do not seek coaches, but do not avoid them. If you indicated to a coach you were going to check on a rule during the game, then do so. If the ruling was correct, explain the ruling. If the ruling was incorrect, then admit your mistake. If a coach approaches you after a game and calmly questions a rule interpretation, hear the coach out. Communication breakdowns between coaches and officials often originate from a basic misunderstanding of the rules.

Communicating with players.

If officials can get the players on their side, they solve one of their biggest problems. When meeting the captains before the game, keep the conversation short. Avoid statements like, "We're the referees tonight" (why else would you be wearing a striped shirt?), and, "We're going to work hard tonight and get the calls right" (if you miss a play, a captain might say, "Hey ref, you lied."). Remind the captains that it is their responsibility to control their team and that if they cannot, then you will take appropriate action. However, let them know that the penalty is much less severe if they control their teammates, than if you have to get involved.

During the game, it is often helpful to respond to any player, not just the captain, who addresses you in a respectful manner. Point guards control the ball and, very often, their team. Point guards, in addition to the designated captain, can be a great help to officials.

Cleaning up post play can be a big problem if you do not communicate with the post players, especially during live-ball periods. Simple terms such as "hands" or "lane" work wonders.

Dead-ball periods are often excellent opportunities to communicate with players. Prior to the opening toss, glance at the clock operator, your partner and the players to make sure they are ready. Then do a little preventive officiating with the jumpers by asking if they are ready and reminding them to hit the ball on its way down.

When administering throw-ins, use the correct terminology. Tell the player it is a spot throw-in if the throw-in is to be made from a designated spot. Do not tell the player he cannot move, because that is not correct by rule, since players can move backward. Stay away from words with too many syllables. Do not tell a player he cannot move laterally. While that may be better terminology than telling a player not to move, you might get a quizzical look for using a multi-syllabic word.

Free throws are excellent opportunities to communicate with players and do preventive officiating. Is post play getting too rough? Is hand-checking a problem? Address it during free throws when you have a captive audience. Do not go to the extreme, though, and conduct a rules clinic or get too verbose.

Sometimes, talking to players does not work in post play, three seconds or hand-checking situations. If preventive officiating is not working, do the next best thing: call the foul or violation. The players eventually figure out the program. Foul calls are very effective forms of communication.

How should you deal with a player taunting after blocking a shot? Penalize it immediately. Talking to a player and asking him not to play defense with his mouth may or may not work. Next you might have to warn the other team if they should taunt, and that next taunt might not warrant a warning. If you do not address taunting swiftly and immediately, it will get worse.

(Steven Ellinger officiates high school and college basketball. He is the director of the Southwest Basketball Referees School at Rice University in Houston and is an IAABO national clinician. These articles first appeared in the 4/01 and 5/01 issues of Referee.)

WHEN SHOULD YOU WHACK 'EM?
By Patrick Rosenow

"To T or not to T?" With apologies to William Shakespeare, that is the question we'll be answering as the basketball season gets started. As the stakes get higher, coaches, players and fans become more frenzied than ever. Unfortunately, that frenzy occasionally turns into hostility as younger players and coaches watch professionals verbally abuse and physically assault officials with little consequence.

Values such as teamwork, discipline, selflessness and respect for your opponents and officials are no longer the primary reason for taking part in sports. They are being replaced with personal accomplishment — usually accompanied by in-your-face taunting or chest-thumping, and crowd-pandering self-aggrandizement.

A few years ago I attended a recertification clinic for FIBA (international basketball) officials. Most of the officials there were accomplished NCAA Division I or NBA referees. One session turned to the topic of bench decorum. The FIBA clinician chided us for the way we indulge abusive coaches. Contrary to what we might think, he said, European officials are trained not to accept such behavior.

"I ask them," he said, "'Are you a good and fair person? Have you worked hard to learn the rules and become a good referee? When you are on the court, are you doing your best to get into position to see the plays correctly? Do you have a favorite team or are you trying to help one side win? Well then, why in the world would you allow someone to curse you or your mother, accuse you of cheating or berate you and try to inflame a group of spectators against you?'"

What he said made sense.

Most of us had never thought about it in exactly those terms. But then one of the better known Division I referees responded that the clinician didn't appreciate the difference between European and U.S. ball. Over here, he pointed out, the abusive coach and the "bad boy" star can be a big part of the "show."

While that attitude exists mostly at the top levels (televised games in particular), its effect is felt all the way down to the high schools and recreational leagues. As for the clinician's example of how the phone-bashing behavior of one well-known Big Ten coach was tolerated, the referee explained that in many such cases, if the coach were assessed a technical foul and ejected, the conference would soon be looking for a new official.

The referee may or may not have been right about major college conferences backing up officials. However, at the high school level in most states, the coach would simply scratch or not rehire the official. Again with a nod to the bard, "There's the rub."

Face it; many referees don't enforce bench decorum rules because they don't want to get scratched by the coach. The most significant motivator for officials is assignments. If you want to make sure an official does something, tell him it will affect how many and what kind of games he'll get.

In one state, the high school athletic association made it absolutely clear that any official not strictly enforcing bench decorum during the state tournament would work no more games. If a coach or player got out of line and you didn't respond, you sat for the rest of the tournament. No explanations would be accepted. When the coaches realized that the referees' desire to continue working the tournament was stronger than their fear of getting scratched, they controlled themselves and their players. In spite of the pressure of the single-elimination tournament, there were very few conduct problems.

It can be done, but first everyone's expectations need changing. Coaches have to realize that officials will enforce the conduct rules. Officials have to have the guts to ignore the possibility that the T they give might mean it's the last game they work for that coach. Likewise, all officials must be consistent. It's a lot easier for Bob to assess a T on Friday night if he can be confident Kathy will do the same thing for the same offense next Tuesday. The key is that if everyone decides mutual respect and sportsmanship are more important than winning (for coaches) or not getting scratched (for officials), courtside tantrums will decrease dramatically.

That's not to say that we shouldn't recognize that basketball is often a highly charged, emotional game. It's just that referees have accepted too much abuse as part of the game that comes with the territory of being an official. Slowly but surely, the threshold of abuse referees accept before responding has risen. In 99.9 percent of the cases where an official regrets a decision involving bench decorum, that official should have assessed a technical foul but didn't. You've done it, and probably used various excuses.

Top six excuses to not give a T.

1. "The coach was begging for it and I wasn't going to give him the satisfaction of getting it." Why a coach violates the rule isn't the point. Once the coach has done enough to warrant a technical, assess it. If you don't, the coach may try to find out just how obnoxious he has to be before you'll have the guts to assert yourself. Remember what the FIBA clinician said. Even if the coach is just trying to pump up the team, what gives that role model the right to use your dignity to do it?

2. "I cut him some slack because we probably missed the call." Most of you have used that one and it might seem to make sense. The problem with it is that the coach thinks you kicked every call he complains about and can't distinguish those very few calls you wish you could have back. Besides, no one will understand why

you'll put up with it one time, but not the next. They'll take your failure to stand up for yourself either as an admission that you blew the call or a sign of weakness. Consistent enforcement is the key in bench decorum just as it is in traveling or contact in the post.

3. "I didn't want to show up my partner." I fell victim to that one last season. In a game between first- (team A) and last- (team B) place teams, team B didn't score in the first quarter. By the third, they were 25 down and my partner had three consecutive block/charge plays right in front of him. From my angle, it looked like the team B defender on plays two and three did exactly what the team A defender had done on play one. Nevertheless, all three calls went against team B. As my partner started to report the third foul, team B's coach stood up, turned to the crowd, yelled something about the call, took his coat off and slammed it on the bench.

Of course, all of that was right in front of my partner. Neither of us did anything about it. I justified my actions in two ways. First, I didn't blame the coach for being mad (see reason number two) and second, if I ran over to take the call from under my partner's nose, it would've just made him look bad. I was wrong. Obviously, it's not a good idea to come from 45 feet away and call a technical on a coach who's standing face-to-face with your partner. On the other hand, that coach, for whatever reason, was out of line. I knew it, the players and fans knew it and the coach knew it. As a result, both my partner and I looked bad.

4. "It was a blowout and I just wanted to get out of there; there was no point in making the game any longer." That was probably another reason we didn't T the coach after the third block/charge call. But again, it wasn't a good reason. The values of sportsmanship and respect for others are just as important in a blowout as in a two-overtime thriller.

5. "It was a close game, the kids had been great and I didn't

want an idiotic comment by a coach to decide it for them." What experienced official hasn't used that rationale for passing on a T? It's flawed, though. First of all, bench decorum is a rule like any other. While no good referee calls a "cheap" three-second or hand-check call with five seconds left in a tie game, you ought to strive for consistency from the first five to the last five minutes of a game. Second, if you ignore flagrantly abusive conduct by the coach because you don't want to affect the outcome, you're saying who wins the game is more important than good sportsmanship and respect.

6. "It just slowly got away from us. We'd let so much go that we'd have looked silly to all of a sudden give a T." That happened to a crew in our association in a district playoff game last season. Fans and off-duty officials in the stands could clearly make out one of the coaches crudely comparing the officiating to barnyard by-products. After the game, the crew said they knew what the coach was saying but had let both benches go to the point that it would not have been fair to pick one coach or another for the first T. The problem: There's no end. They started off with good intentions by hoping the benches would calm down, but it didn't happen. They only made the situation worse by not stepping up and doing what they should have a quarter earlier.

Clearly, sports officials are under siege. As television shows officials headbutted, spit at, cursed and on the receiving end of obscene gestures, fans and players may come to believe that officials are paid to take the abuse. We aren't.

Properly enforcing sportsmanship is not about coming out with an attitude and pulling the trigger whenever a coach complains about a call. It is about meeting the responsibility to give a technical foul when it's deserved. After all, there is a fine but important line between allowing a coach to vent some understandable frustration and not demanding the same respect referees show the coach. If you're afraid to draw that line, you're hurting the game and the great things it stands for. When that happens — with a final apology to William — "the fault lies not in our (basketball) stars, but in ourselves."

(Written by Pat Rosenow, a United States Air Force trial judge from Woodbridge, Va. Rosenow started refereeing basketball in 1976 and currently works mostly at the high school level. He has served as clinician and interpreter for various associations and has been FIBA-certified since 1984. This article first appeared in the 4/97 issue of Referee.)

JACK MADDEN: 'TECHNICAL' LESSONS FROM AN NBA LEGEND

The way you call a technical foul is as important as calling the technical foul. Jack Madden, a retired 30-year NBA referee, learned that valuable lesson early in his professional career.

Many remember Madden for his smooth, fluid mechanics and his calm demeanor. He says the latter was not always the case.

"I called 89 technical fouls in one season," said Madden. That 1970-71 season, Madden said many people were trying to get him fired because of it.

Despite the perceptions associated with his technical-foul total, Madden was assigned to the NBA Finals, working game three and serving as an alternate for the final game. Ed Rush and Richie Powers worked as Milwaukee beat Baltimore for the championship.

After the game, Madden went out for dinner with Rush, Powers and NBA supervisor of officials John Nucatola. It was that postgame dinner conversation that may have saved Jack Madden's career.

"There was an incident that occurred during the game," said

Madden. "(Baltimore's) Jack Marin got really upset with a call Ed Rush made, but Ed turned his back and walked away and didn't hit him with a technical. Nucatola said to Ed, 'You used great discretion out there on the court tonight in not calling a technical foul on Marin. Thank goodness Jack Madden wasn't working the game. He probably would have ejected him.'"

Madden was troubled by the statement, but waited for a better time to discuss it with Nucatola. On the way to the hotel, Madden seized a private moment with his supervisor and asked what he meant by the comment. Nucatola said to Madden, "Well, Jack, you know how you are. At the tip of a hat you're going to call a technical foul. And you know, Jack, I've gone to bat for you this year and I think I've been able to save your job. That's how close you've come to getting fired."

The conversation continued. Nucatola asked Madden if he was aware he called 89 technicals that year. Madden said he was not aware — he didn't keep a count. And he said to Nucatola, "I can assure you that most of those technical fouls were called because my partners were new to the league, they had lost control of the games and I was in charge and that was the way I was keeping control of games."

> **"Thank goodness Jack Madden wasn't working the game. He probably would have ejected him."**

Nucatola's response changed the way Madden officiated forever. The supervisor said, "Well, I understand that but Ed Rush had 86 technicals. He was only three behind you but nobody said anything about Ed. It was your demeanor, the way you call those technicals. You had this look on your face like you were going to bite somebody's head off. You know what I want you to do next year? I want you to go out there next year and before you call a technical foul, I want you to count to three and ask yourself, 'Can I avoid this technical foul?' If you can, you've saved a technical foul and you'll find yourself a better referee for it."

Madden now says, "That's the best advice I ever got as a professional basketball referee. The next year, I went from 89 technicals to 30. (Nucatola) said to me that night, 'Jack, you're as good as any referee on our staff mechanically, your positioning, your judgment, everything. The thing I want you to work on is your demeanor on the floor. If you can correct that, you'll be our number-one guy.'"

As Madden became a veteran, many younger officials complimented him about his demeanor and asked how he always stayed in control when he called a technical. "I always tell them my John Nucatola story," he said. "After he talked to me, my whole attitude and demeanor changed. I knew that I was going to be in control of the game and if I had to call a technical foul, I wasn't going to show any anger at all. Or if a guy came up to me and started screaming and yelling at me, I wasn't going to scream and yell back because that only compounds the problem. All I would do is try to be as cool as I could and then when he was done (yelling at me), I would hit him with a technical foul and walk away. It really worked because it kind of settled the player or coach down."

Madden says the same philosophy holds true in everyday life. An avid golfer, Madden used a golfing analogy to illustrate his point. He said that if you hit a bad golf shot and start getting angry, your emotions negatively impact your next shot. "It affects the next shot, and so on, then you're really angry and pretty soon you've ruined the whole round. The same holds true for refereeing. If you get angry, you're going to carry it through your next call and so on. I learned a valuable lesson from John Nucatola that night. I've tried to carry it throughout my life in everything I do."

(This article first appeared in the 7/96 issue of Referee.*)*

6

Tips, Techniques and Suggestions

What do we mean by tips? Referee uses the term to pass along some small tidbit of knowledge that usually isn't found in a formal mechanics manual. It's something that is passed word-of-mouth from mentor to referee being mentored.

These tips may save you a few steps or they may improve your game control. You won't use every tip every game. But put each tool in your toolbag and know that it's there when you need it.

SIX TIPS FOR USING THE WHISTLE

When most people consider communicating, they think of talking. There are many other ways to communicate — like body language and signals — that you use every time you're on the court. One tool that you use that doesn't always get a lot of consideration is your whistle. It is an important part of communication.

The whistle is a communication tool. It's really just an extension of your voice and your signals. Blowing the whistle loudly has the same impact of you screaming; blowing the whistle softly equates to whispering. A "normal" whistle blow is as if you were talking in a normal tone of voice.

1. Sharp blast when stopping the clock.
When stopping the clock (using either the open-hand or closed-fist overhead signals), simultaneously use a sharp, strong whistle blast. There's no need to blow the whistle many times with short blasts; that doesn't communicate anything of substance and draws unnecessary attention to the call. Officials who blow the whistle many times while making a single call are generally showboating.

2. Substitutions: Do what your supervisor wants.
Blowing the whistle while beckoning in a substitute is debatable.

Some supervisors want officials to blow their whistle when beckoning all substitutes. Why? The whistle gets the attention of the substitute and the official's partner, letting both know the substitution is taking place.

Other supervisors don't want officials blowing the whistle when beckoning in substitutes. Why? Blowing the whistle is demonstrative and draws attention to the official. Plus, with good signals and eye contact, the whistle isn't needed.

Here might be the most obvious *Referee* recommendation we've published in awhile: Do what your supervisor wants. If there is no supervisor or no decision on what method to use, *Referee* recommends blowing the whistle only when there is some confusion as to when the substitute may enter or when the substitute can't hear your voice or see your signals.

3. Use a longer whistle on timeouts.

When a team requests and is granted a timeout, use a slightly longer whistle while signaling the timeout. That longer whistle distinguishes a timeout from a normal whistle blast that stops the clock.

4. Slow down on double whistles.

Some plays have both officials briefly watching the same player. That's especially true with on-ball coverage in a halfcourt setting in the lane area. Sometimes both officials blow the whistle at the same time. By following the correct procedure, you'll avoid the embarrassment and confusion of having one official signaling one thing and the other signaling something else at the same time.

There's a general rule for double whistles: If the play is moving toward you, you have the call. If the play is moving away from you, you give the call up to your partner.

Following correct signal procedures is critical with double whistles. If you don't, you'll probably have an unwanted double call. It's important to take the time to use the correct signal to stop the clock (either open hand or fist overhead, depending on the call) and simultaneously blow your whistle. If you hear your partner's whistle, quickly make eye contact before signaling anything else. You and your partner will likely need to penetrate on the play and quickly tell each other what you've got. Again, in most cases, the official who the play is moving toward likely takes the call.

An exception is if the official who has the play moving away has a foul or violation that occurred before the partner's whistle.

Understand that most double whistles occur in the lane area. When you make a call in that area, expect that there might be a double whistle and quickly glance at your partner before signaling the type of foul or violation. Knowing where double whistles tend to occur helps when you can't hear your partner's whistle because of crowd noise or the noise of your own whistle.

5. Blow it louder to help sell a call.

Use your whistle to your advantage. Think of it as an extension of your voice. Blow it louder than normal when you really need to sell something. Use a strong, short blast in most situations.

6. A soft whistle means a soft call.

Avoid blowing a soft whistle. Just like soft signals that aren't crisp and clear, soft whistles convey that you're not sure about what you've called. Make sure your whistle blasts exude confidence and control without going overboard.

GLANCE AT THE CLOCK

Clock malfunctions and timing errors can be an officiating nightmare; they don't have to be.

Each time a whistle blows to stop the game clock, quickly

glance at the clock to see the time. Before checking, however, make sure players' actions are under control; you don't want to look away from the players if there's a problem.

All officials should glance. In fact, the off-ball official(s) may have a better chance to look quickly since they're not involved with action around the ball. NCAA officials should also check the shot clock.

Also glance at the clock just before allowing the ball to become live. Obviously, the time on the clock when the ball became dead should be the same when the ball next becomes live. By gathering clock information, you are fully prepared if the clock malfunctions or time is run off the clock — accidentally or intentionally. It takes some discipline to develop that good habit, but once accomplished, glancing at the clock becomes second-nature. Your efforts will pay off the first time you correctly handle a clock problem with confidence.

THREE TIPS FOR THE TRAIL

There's an old adage that rings true: In a two-person game, if the trail works hard and has a good game, the crew will have a good game. A solid trail official moves aggressively to get good angles and helps the lead on rebounding. Here are three tips that will improve your game as a trail official:

1. Get an inside-out look. With a crew of two officials, the trail official often has to get off the sideline and move toward the center of the court to officiate action on the far side of the floor. When that happens, the trail can get caught in the middle on a swing pass from one side of the court to the other. Adjustments must be made.

A simple one or two step adjustment toward the center of the court gives you the proper angle. You must fight the urge to run around the entire play toward the sideline, using six steps or more and wasting precious time. By the time you run around the play, the offensive player could take a shot (was the shooter's foot on or behind the three-point arc?), violate or be fouled — and you may not have seen it.

2. Move off the sideline. Effective court coverage requires significant movement by the trail.

When an offensive player has the ball on the side of the floor opposite the trail, the trail must move away from the near sideline and get proper angles. By staying too close to the near sideline, the trail cannot effectively see action near the ball and must make judgments from a distance — way too far away to convince anyone the trail saw the play correctly.

Avoid moving straight toward the play: You could interfere with the play by stepping into a passing lane. Take an angle toward the division line to decrease your chances of interfering with the play. In extreme cases, you may even position yourself in the backcourt.

3. Pick up the shooter on a skip pass. In two-person mechanics, the lead official should move to the ball side of the lane when the player with the ball is below the free-throw line extended and a potential post pass is evident.

Though ball side mechanics are effective for controlling post play, one weakness is coverage of a skip pass to the opposite wing player for a quick shot.

Though the opposite wing player is primarily observed by the lead official (even though the lead moved ball side), when a skip pass occurs the trail should adjust a step or two toward the wing player (to the center of the floor) and get a good angle to rule on three-point attempts, fouls and possibly obvious out-of-bounds infractions. Though a long distance look, that's better than having the lead guess because the lead's looking through lane traffic or sprinting head-down to the other side of the court and missing the banging going on in the post.

JUDGE GOALTENDING CORRECTLY

Goaltending is arguably one of the most difficult calls in basketball. It can get officials in trouble for a couple of reasons:

1. It doesn't happen very often (especially during high school and lower level games).

2. Officials are usually not watching the ball after it has been released on a try.

In almost all situations, in a two-person crew the trail is responsible for goaltending. However, the lead can call goaltending if the trail doesn't see it. That's very rare because the lead shouldn't be watching the flight of the ball from the endline; the lead should be watching strong-side rebounding, etc. Another exception: When the trail moving to new lead on a transition play is behind the fastbreak play, the new lead has primary goaltending responsibility.

Because goaltending is somewhat rare, it becomes a reactionary call that can take you by surprise. Too often the trail is correctly watching other things: fouls in the act of shooting, three-point lines, fouls after the try has been released, weak-side rebounding, etc. When a defensive player leaps to block the shot, an official's reaction is sometimes just a bit slow, reducing judgment to guesswork.

To correctly rule on goaltending, you must judge the arc of the ball. That's easier said than done because of all the other things you have to observe. In theory it's simple: ball is upward, no-call; ball is downward, goaltending. The reality is much different, especially when the ball is near its apex, or the top of the arc. The short- to medium-range jump shots are most difficult, generally because they happen so quickly.

One simple tool officials can use to help themselves judge goaltending correctly is knowing where the defender is in relation to the shooter and the basket. Simply stated, if the defender is closer to the shooter than to the basket when the ball is touched, you've likely got a no-call because the ball is likely still on its way up. If the defender is closer to the basket than to the shooter when the ball is touched, it's probably goaltending because the ball is likely on its way down.

JUDGE THE PASS/CRASH

A player driving a crowded lane, passing off to a teammate, then crashing into a defender is an especially difficult play to officiate in a two-person crew. Why? There's a lot going on in a small area in a short period of time.

For the lead, the play is especially tough to handle alone. Did the passer get fouled? Did the passer foul? Block? Charge? Did the passer foul after releasing the ball or was it a player-control foul? Did the dribbler travel? Did the player filling the lane catch the pass cleanly and travel or did the player merely fumble and recover? Did the violation occur before the foul?

The trail must help. By aggressively penetrating toward the endline when players drive the lane, the trail can take some of the pressure off the lead by being in great position to judge the play.

The common phrase that sums up responsibilities is, "Lead takes the pass, trail takes the crash." That's generally accurate when the pass is toward the lead. However, when the pass is toward the trail (especially out toward the perimeter), the trail should take the pass and the lead take the crash.

The trail should watch the dribbler penetrate. Watch for the dribbler being fouled on the drive or fouled while passing.

Also, the trail watches for the dribbler crashing into a defender after releasing a pass that goes toward the lead. Referee the defense to see if the defender obtained legal guarding position. Be especially wary of dribblers who leave their feet to make a pass. Don't bail out an out-of-control player by making a no-call.

Whatever call is made and whoever makes it, sell it! It's a real "bang-bang" play that can have major implications. For example, if the dribbler goes airborne to make the pass, the player filling the lane catches the pass and is about to lay it in when the airborne player crashes into a defender, that foul wipes away the basket. The trail must have the intestinal fortitude to come in strong and make that call.

KEEP COACHES IN THE COACHING BOXES

In many pregame conversations, referees often forget to talk about the people they have to deal with, in this case, the coaches and assistant coaches. In many games, how you handle those coaches will dictate how the game will flow. Deal with them professionally and you've given them a chance deal with you professionally. Back them into a corner and you're asking them for a fight. In most cases, the way you deal with them is more important than what is actually said.

With that in mind, here's a list of ways to deal with coaches, excerpted from *You're In Charge: 104 Ways to Better Manage Your Games*, a *Referee* publication.

Head coaches.

1. Make eye contact. A coach wants to be assured that he has your attention. Don't act distracted.

2. Never call coaches by their first names. They'll feel most comfortable, particularly in front of their players, simply by being called "coach."

3. Show respect to get respect. That means using formal

language, keeping communication brief, adopting a neutral tone and avoiding any personal remarks. Stick to the issue at hand in a straightforward way.

4. Ask them to deal with problem players. Be sure to identify the problem in explicit terms, without making the player to be an evil person.

5. Remain calm under all circumstances. If a coach moves toward you to "get in your face," pivot sideways so that you are shoulder-to-shoulder. It is hard for someone to speak in an aggressive, confrontational way when the proximity between parties is side-by-side.

6. Let coaches have their say. When a coach approaches to protest or argue, adopt an instant "listening mode" and let the aggrieved individual finish his or her remarks. Do not interrupt.

7. Use non-confrontational body language. To be aware of body posture, facial expressions, head tilt and arm positions, one must say, "I am going to appear receptive and contemplative. I can think best and measure my words that way. I am determined not to escalate the problem."

8. If you make a mistake, admit it. A simple apology is sufficient; do not elaborate or rationalize (i.e., make excuses).

9. When coaches raise their voice, lower yours. A soft voice has a way of triggering a reciprocal soft reply.

10. Get both coaches together. Sometimes there is a need to reach a uniform agreement in a joint consultation. Issues could include clock problems or difficulties with game equipment.

11. Support fellow officials. Never betray partners by showing that you doubt their judgment. Instead indicate faith in someone else's decision by saying the partner had a better view or a more favorable angle.

12. Acknowledge the coach: "I hear what you're saying." "I understand" or "I see what you mean" are equally effective. If the next sensible step is to confer with a partner over a

controversy, make that next move firmly.

13. Give praise when proper; promote sportsmanship. When a coach makes a gesture of consideration for the opponents or toward the officials, be sure to acknowledge it. Sometimes a smile and a nod of the head are enough.

14. Determine where the coach is coming from. Put yourself in their shoes just as you would in trying to understand a player's viewpoint. Sometimes how the coach will be viewed in the eyes of players and team supporters is the primary stimulus for behavior.

15. Keep your ego under control. Often a mere glance will carry a significant message, whether it's negative or positive, whether it is meant to curtail dialogue or to encourage it. A quizzical expression can signal a desire for additional input, whereas a frown may denote closure.

16. Give the coach the benefit of the doubt, but be sure there is doubt. If you are uncertain about the accuracy of a ruling, make a decision and tell the coach what you believe is correct.

17. Permit the coach to disengage. Recognize (through facial expression, body language and terminating vocal patterns) when it is time to cease a dialogue.

18. Don't use your hands when talking to a coach. Your gestures will reveal more than you'll want to convey.

Assistant coaches.

1. Remind the head coach that he or she is responsible for the assistants. It might be best to do that after a game starts if the assistants become argumentative. If you do that before the game, it might cause the coach to become defensive, unless you state it in positive terms, such as, "We'd like to deal with you exclusively when questions arise."

2. Deal with assistants directly. Treat them with equal respect, as you would players and the head coach. If there is a legitimate complaint, treat it seriously.

3. Don't fraternize. If a coach is an acquaintance, shift into a formal mode and operate as though a friendship were not applicable.

4. Give parameters ahead of time. Sometimes an assistant is tuned in to play concerns and injuries more than the head coach. If so, use the assistant as a liaison or conduit for such information.

5. Don't assume negatives. An assistant may not automatically be an antagonist. Take an approach which emphasizes positive feelings such as asking the assistant coach to identify things you may not have noticed, a player who is frustrated and upset, for instance.

IF YOU LIKE THIS BOOK, YOU'LL LOVE THIS MAGAZINE!

The only magazine exclusively for sports officials

Rulings, caseplays, mechanics – in-depth

Solid coverage of the sport(s) you work

Important, late-breaking news stories

Thought-provoking interviews and features

Opinions/editorials on vital topics

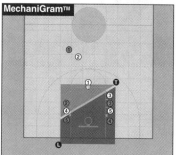

All Sports
All Levels
Always
There For You **NAS○**

The National Association of Sports Officials

- NASO's "Members Only Edition" of *Referee* magazine every month. Members receive 96-pages of *Referee* with 16-pages of association news, "members only" tips, case plays and ducational product discounts.

- Members receive a *FREE* educational publication valued up to $9.95.

- Discounts on NASO/*Referee* publications such as the Officials' Guidebooks, rules comparisons and sport-specific preseason publications make you a better official.

- Referral service in the event you move to another community.

- Web page and e-mail communications keep you updated on NASO news, services and benefits.

- "Ask Us" rules interpretations service.

- Sports-specific rules quizzes.

- Free NASO e-mail address.

- Free access to the *NASO LockerRoom* — an NASO cyberspace service.

- Membership Certificate and laminated membership card.

- NASO Code of Ethics.

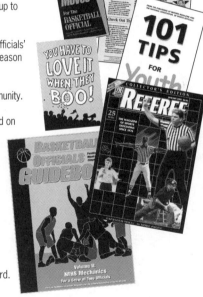

For a complete brochure and membership information contact:
NASO • 2017 Lathrop Avenue • Racine, WI 53405
262/632-5448 • 262/632-5460 (fax)
naso@naso.org or visit our website at www.naso.org